POPULAR SONGS
HAL LEONARD
STUDENT PIANO LIBRARY

Classical Pop

Lady Gaga Fugue and Other Pop Hits Arranged in Classical Style

Arranged by Giovanni Dettori

CONTENTS

ISBN 978-1-4584-6561-0

HAL•LEONARD®
CORPORATION
7777 W. BLUEMOUND RD. P.O. BOX 13819 MILWAUKEE, WI 53213

Visit Hal Leonard Online at
www.halleonard.com

100 Years
(Two-part Invention)

Words and Music by
John Ondrasik
Arranged by Giovanni Dettori

Moderato (♩ = 60)

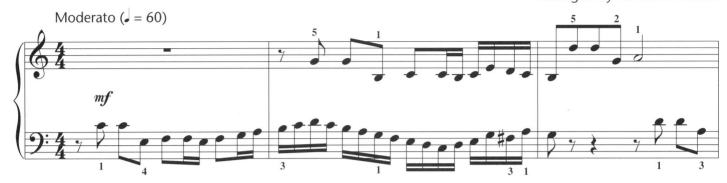

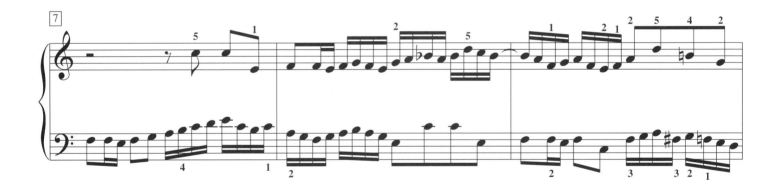

3

Don't Know Why
(French Style)

Words and Music by
Jesse Harris
Arranged by Giovanni Dettori

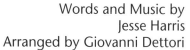

Hey Jude
(Theme and Variations)

Words and Music by
John Lennon and Paul McCartney
Arranged by Giovanni Dettori

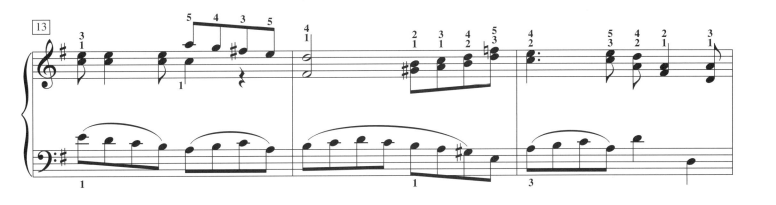

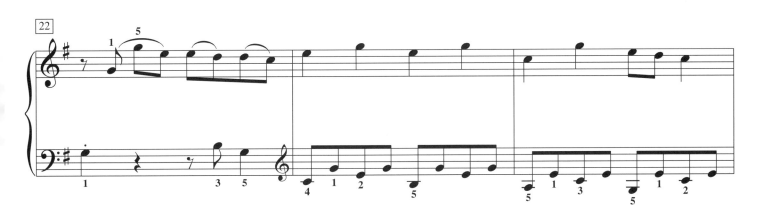

VARIATION II
Adagio (♩ = 72)

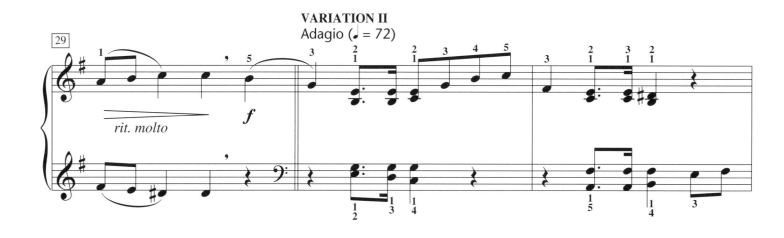

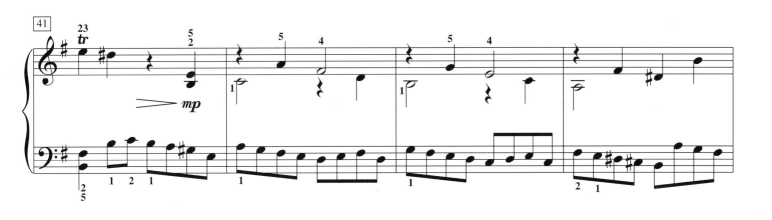

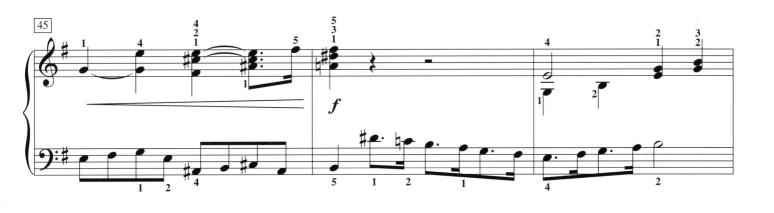

VARIATION III
Adagio (♩ = 72)

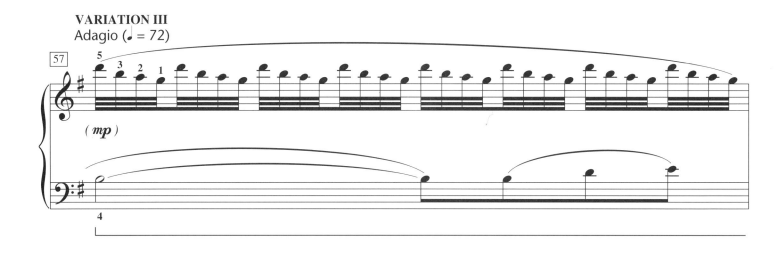

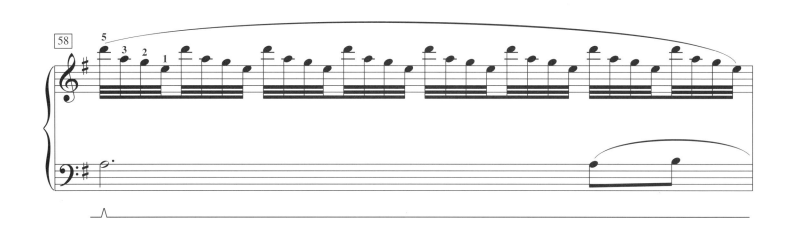

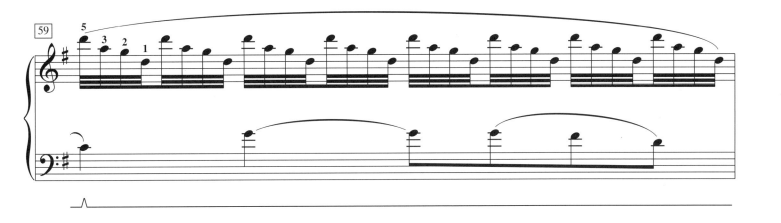

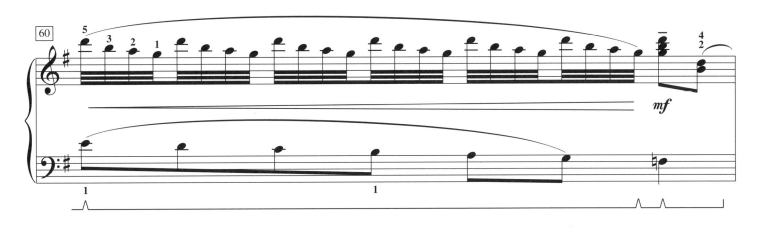

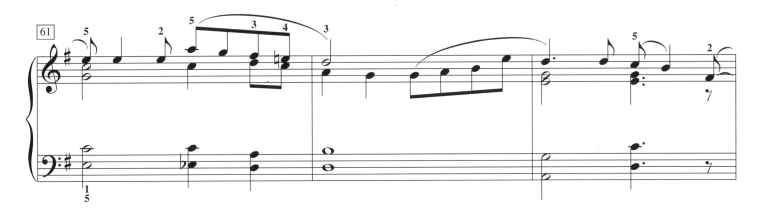

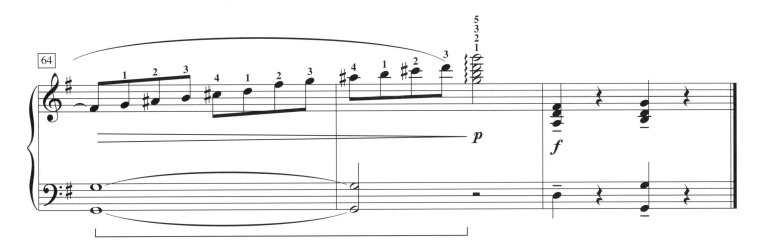

Just the Way You Are

(Romantic Style)

Words and Music by Bruno Mars,
Ari Levine, Philip Lawrence,
Khari Cain and Khalil Walton
Arranged by Giovanni Dettori

14

Lady Gaga Fugue

(Based on the song *Bad Romance*)

Words and Music by Stefani Germanotta
and Nadir Khayat
Arranged by Giovanni Dettori

Moderato (♩ = 96)

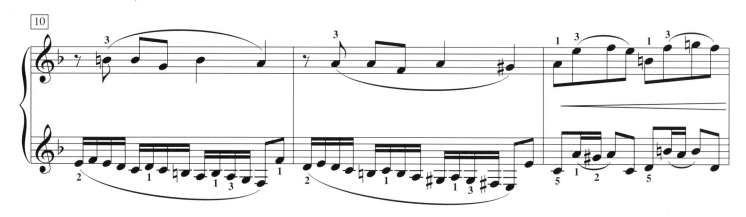

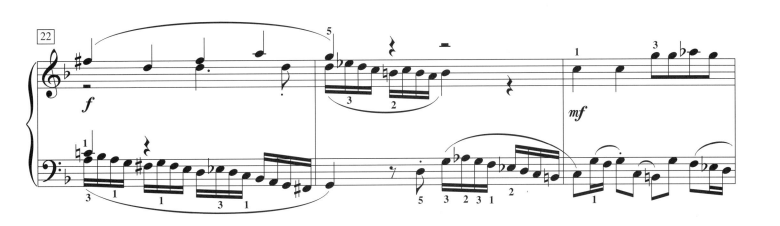

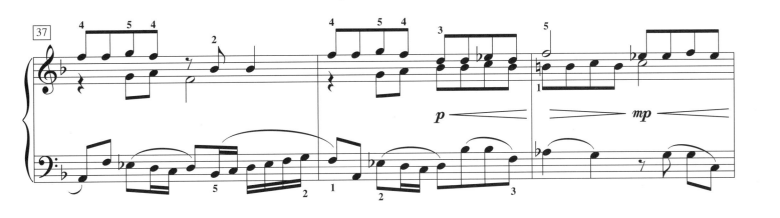

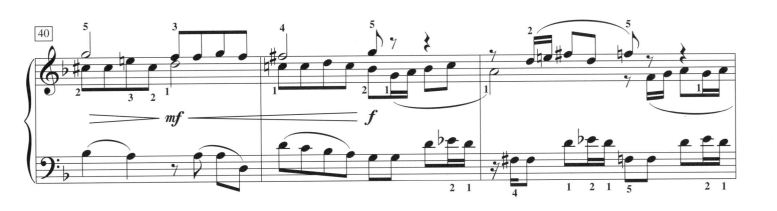

Never Say Never

from THE KARATE KID

(Nocturne)

Words and Music by Justin Bieber,
Nasri Atweh, Thaddis Harrell,
Omarr Rambert, Adam Messinger
and Jaden Smith
Arranged by Giovanni Dettori

22

My Heart Will Go On

(Love Theme From 'Titanic')

from the Paramount and Twentieth Century Fox Motion Picture TITANIC

(Sonatina)

Music by James Horner
Lyric by Will Jennings
Arranged by Giovanni Dettori

Teenage Dream
(Impromptu)

Words and Music by Lukasz Gottwald,
Max Martin, Benjamin Levin,
Bonnie McKee and Katy Perry
Arranged by Giovanni Dettori

R.H. over

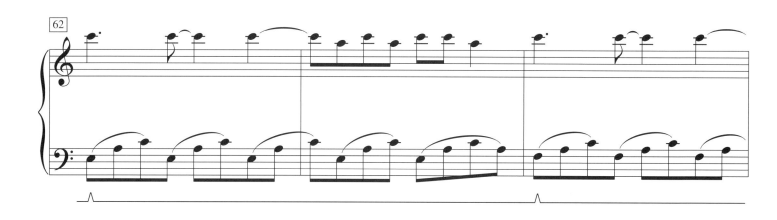

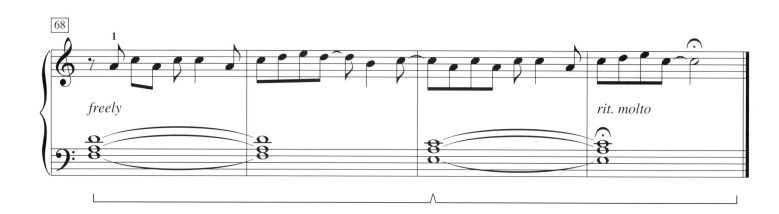